AF269507

ITALY

BY CARLA MOONEY

Essential Library

An Imprint of Abdo Publishing
abdobooks.com

ABDOBOOKS.COM

Published by Abdo Publishing, a division of ABDO, PO Box 398166, Minneapolis, Minnesota 55439. Copyright © 2023 by Abdo Consulting Group, Inc. International copyrights reserved in all countries. No part of this book may be reproduced in any form without written permission from the publisher. Essential Library™ is a trademark and logo of Abdo Publishing.

Printed in the United States of America, North Mankato, Minnesota.
102022
012023

Cover Photos: Viacheslav Lopatin/Shutterstock Images (Sant'Angelo bridge); Tetiana Denysenko/Shutterstock Images, (pattern)
Interior Photos: Paolo Gallo/Shutterstock Images, 4–5, 38–39; Nicola Forenza/Shutterstock Images, 6, 9; Lukas Gojda/Shutterstock Images, 8; Claudio Giovanni Colombo/Shutterstock Images, 11; Shutterstock Images, 12, 14–15, 18, 19, 28, 34, 41, 46, 47, 63, 73, 90, 101; Peter Hermes Furian/Shutterstock Images, 17 (Italy); Web Tools/Shutterstock Images, 17 (globe); Da Liu/Shutterstock Images, 22–23; Gary Yeowell/Digital Vision/Getty Images, 26–27; Antonello Vercelli/Eye Em/Getty Images, 30–31; Simone Capponi/Shutterstock Images, 36–37; David Pineda Svenske/Shutterstock Images, 40; Davide Zanin Photography/Shutterstock Images, 42; Science Source/Photo Researchers History/Archive Photos/Getty Images, 44; Everett Collection/Shutterstock Images, 48; Michael Regan/UEFA/Getty Images Sports/Getty Images, 52–53; Alex Segre/Shutterstock Images, 55; Lisa Maree Williams/Getty Images News/Getty Images, 56; NurPhoto/Getty Images, 59; Fine Art Images/Heritage Images/Hulton Fine Art Collection/Getty Images, 60; Casimiro PT/Shutterstock Images, 61; Gianni Pasquini/Alamy, 65; Fabrizio Maffei/Shutterstock Images, 66–67; Alessandro Di Meo/AM Pool/Getty Images News/Getty Images, 69; Giorgio Cosulich/Getty Images News/Getty Images, 70; Alexander A. Nedviga/Shutterstock Images, 75; Antonio Masiello/Getty Images News/Getty Images, 76–77; Miguel Medina/AFP/Getty Images, 78–79; Alberto Pizzoli/AFP/Getty Images, 83; iStockphoto, 84, 86, 88–89; Laura Lezza/Getty Images News/Getty Images, 94; Elisabetta A. Villa/Getty Images Entertainment/Getty Images, 96; Marco Di Lauro/Getty Images News/Getty Images, 97

Editor: Priscilla An
Series Designer: Maggie Villaume

Library of Congress Control Number: 2022940384

PUBLISHER'S CATALOGING-IN-PUBLICATION DATA

Names: Mooney, Carla, author.
Title: Italy / by Carla Mooney
Description: Minneapolis, Minnesota: Abdo Publishing, 2023 | Series: Essential Library of Countries | Includes online resources and index.
Identifiers: ISBN 9781532199448 (lib. bdg.) | ISBN 9781098274641 (ebook)
Subjects: LCSH: Italy--Juvenile literature. | Europe--Juvenile literature. | Italy--History--Juvenile literature. | Geography--Juvenile literature.
Classification: DDC 954.0--dc23

CONTENTS

A TOUR OF ITALY

"**B**envenuti a Roma! Welcome to Rome!" the flight attendant announces as the plane touches down on the runway at Fiumicino Airport outside Rome, Italy. After picking up their suitcases, Alicia and her mom catch a taxi to their hotel in the historic center of Rome. On this late December day, almost every storefront and door they pass shines with wreaths, garlands, and lights to celebrate the Christmas season.

Entering the hotel lobby, Alicia takes in the soaring ceilings, period furniture, elegant fabrics, and oil paintings that decorate the spacious rooms. A towering Christmas tree sparkles with white lights, spreading its

Rome is the capital of Italy and has more than four million inhabitants.

The Colosseum is one of Italy's best-known monuments.

warm glow throughout the lobby. Alicia and her mother have traveled across the Atlantic Ocean from the United States to Italy to celebrate her cousin's wedding. Before the ceremony, Alicia and her mother have planned several days of sightseeing to enjoy the rich culture and history of this southern European country.

AN ANCIENT AMPHITHEATER

The sightseeing begins the following day with a visit to one of Rome's most iconic sites, the Colosseum. The massive amphitheater has been a part of Rome's history for nearly 2,000 years, with the structure's construction beginning in the year 72 CE and finishing in 80 CE when Emperor Titus ruled the Roman Empire. The completed amphitheater measured 617 feet (188 m) long, 512 feet (156 m) wide, and 187 feet (57 m) tall.[1]

First known as the Flavian Amphitheatre, the Colosseum hosted more than 50,000 spectators for various events.[2] Exhibitions of exotic animals, prisoner executions, gladiator fights, and battle re-creations entertained the Romans for several hundred years. The last recorded games held in the Colosseum occurred in the 500s.

Long after live events had ended at the Colosseum, the amphitheater served other purposes and was used as a storehouse, church, cemetery, and castle. Over the years, it has endured lootings, earthquakes, and even bombings during World War II (1939–1945). Today, the Colosseum is one of Rome's most recognizable tourist attractions, and approximately six million tourists visit it annually.[3]

Alicia enters the Colosseum through the Gladiator's Gate, where ancient Roman fighters entered the building centuries ago. She listens intently as the guide brings to life the stories of the people who lived and died in the amphitheater. On the arena floor, Alicia stops and gazes into the stands. She imagines what it felt like to be a fighter battling a wild animal or another gladiator while the crowd of spectators thundered their approval.

WALKING IN PIAZZA NAVONA

After exploring Rome's ancient history, Alicia and her mother head over to Piazza Navona, which is crowded with shoppers, tourists, and locals. A piazza is a public square or marketplace. Piazza Navona is one of the largest piazzas in Rome and is home to three magnificent fountains. As she walks through the piazza, Alicia stops to admire one of the fountains, the Fontana dei Quattro Fiumi, a name meaning "The Fountain of Four Rivers." The fountain was built in 1651 and features a tall Roman obelisk at its center. Positioned around the obelisk, four figures represent the world's great rivers, the Ganges, Nile, Danube, and Rio de la Plata. The fountain was built for Pope Innocent X and displays the Pope's coat of arms, featuring a dove and an olive branch, on the fountain's base.

Many restaurants surround the Piazza Navona, and street artists, painters, and musicians create a lively atmosphere in the square. Alicia follows her mother to an address near the square. They ring the doorbell and are ushered into the building.

LEANING TOWER OF PISA

One of Italy's most iconic architectural sites is the Leaning Tower of Pisa. The tower's construction began in 1173 and took about 200 years to complete. Built with white marble, the tower was designed to rise 185 feet (56 m) tall and have eight stories including the bell chamber.[5] The tower's stories are ringed by 207 columns.[6] Today, the tower leans to the side due to uneven settling of its foundation in the soft ground. The tower's top tilts about 17 feet (5.2 m) off center.[7] Over the years, various architects have tried to keep it from leaning more. In the 1920s, the tower's foundations were injected with cement grout, which helped stabilize it.

Piazza Navona is a vibrant and historic public square in Rome. It has an unusual oval shape because it used to be a stadium for athletic games.

It's time to participate in another Italian tradition and join several other people for a traditional Italian pasta-making class.

LEARNING TO MAKE PASTA

Alicia puts on an apron, washes her hands, and enjoys a welcome drink and antipasto. She listens closely as the instructor demonstrates each step of the recipes while sharing funny stories and fascinating facts about Italy. First, the class learns how to make tiramisu by dipping ladyfingers into a rich coffee and layering them with a mixture of eggs and cream. They top off the dessert with a sprinkle of cocoa and then put it aside to rest.

Next, the group prepares fresh pasta dough from scratch. Alicia helps mix and knead the pasta dough, which takes a lot of effort and muscle. They run the dough through a roller and shape it to create fettuccine and ravioli. Next, the group prepares two sauces, a fresh marinara and a garlic butter sauce. The chef jokes with the group and gives them a few tips to peel garlic easily. Then, he cooks the pasta, and the group sits down to enjoy their hard work. Alicia's stomach rumbles as the chef places a steaming plate of ravioli in front of her. It is delicious, and she can't believe she helped make it. She soaks up the sauce with a large piece of fresh bread until her plate is empty. She finishes the meal

with her tiramisu and hopes that the espresso in the delicious dessert will give her an after-lunch energy boost.

VINEYARDS IN THE ITALIAN COUNTRYSIDE

After lunch, Alicia and her mother drive a rental car into the Italian countryside. They stop at Casale del Marchese, a winery in Italy's Lazio region. The winery boasts more than 124 acres (50 ha) of grapevines and ancient olive trees in the foothills of an ancient volcano.[9] The property's villa was built in the 1700s on top of two ancient Roman cisterns, and the Carletti family has been running the winery for centuries. Alicia and her mother join a tour of the property and walk through the vineyards and historic wine cellars, listening to their guide explain the wine-making process.

After the vineyard tour, Alicia and her mother drive back to Rome. They have a wedding rehearsal dinner to attend tonight at a restaurant called Da Pancrazio. Alicia is looking forward to it, as she has learned the restaurant was built over the ruins of the Theatre of Pompey, the site where Rome's famous leader Julius Caesar was murdered in 44 BCE. She is fascinated by the chance to stand in the same spot where history took place.

As she changes her clothes for the rehearsal dinner, Alicia plans some of the other sights and activities that she wants to experience in Rome and Italy. At the top of her list is a trip to Vatican City to explore Saint Peter's Basilica, the Vatican museums, and the Sistine Chapel. Vatican City is an independent city-state in the middle of Rome. It is the headquarters of the Roman Catholic Church and home of the Pope. It is also home to many world-famous artworks. Alicia has studied famous artists such as Michelangelo and Raphael at school and can't wait to see their art in person.

AN ICONIC DESTINATION

Visitors from around the world travel to Italy every year. From the Alps to the Mediterranean Sea, Italy attracts people of all ages and interests. The country is known for its rich history, outgoing people, and delectable food. It sits on a peninsula that reaches into the Mediterranean Sea, and its shape is often compared to a boot. Its capital city, Rome, is the home of art masterpieces and ancient ruins. Other major cities include Florence, Venice, and Milan. In 2022, about 60 million people lived in Italy.[10]

With roots reaching back to the Roman Empire, Italy is one of Europe's earliest civilizations. Visitors can enjoy iconic pieces of the country's more than 2,000-year history at museums, archaeological sites, and ancient buildings that still stand in Italy's major cities today. Beyond its major cities, Italy boasts magnificent mountains, peaceful lakes, and Mediterranean beaches. A country with a rich history and vibrant culture, Italy is one of the world's top travel destinations. As the Italians say, when in Italy, *la vita e bella*! Life is beautiful!

POMPEII

One of Italy's most popular tourist destinations, the ancient city of Pompeii is an archaeological site in southern Italy's Campania region. In 79 CE, the nearby volcano Vesuvius erupted and buried the Roman city under several feet of ash, lava, and rock. Many of the city's residents died in their homes, while others suffocated from the fumes of the volcanic gases. The thick covering of ash preserved much of the town, and today visitors can explore the excavated ruins of streets and houses.

CHAPTER TWO

GEOGRAPHY

Located in southern Europe, Italy boasts a variety of memorable landscapes. Rugged mountain ranges flatten into rolling hills across the country, while crystal blue waters meet fine sandy beaches on the coast. From mountains and volcanoes to lakes and coastal regions, Italy is a breathtaking destination that many people hope to visit in their lifetimes.

A BOOT-SHAPED PENINSULA

Italy sits on a peninsula that reaches into the Mediterranean Sea. Parts of the Mediterranean surround Italy on three sides, with the Adriatic Sea to the east, the Tyrrhenian Sea to the west, and the Ionian

Many travelers visit Lago di Braies, a picture-perfect lake nestled among the Dolomite mountains. People can rent wooden rowboats to see the sights.

Sea to the south. West of the peninsula are the islands of Sicily and Sardinia. Italy is bordered by France, Switzerland, Austria, and Slovenia to the north. The country's location has played an important role in its history.

Italy's elongated shape is often compared to a tall boot, and the country is sometimes called "the boot." Italy's Puglia region in the southeast is known as the heel of the boot, while the Calabria region in the southwest is called the toe of the boot.

Italy's land covers 116,350 square miles (301,340 sq km), including Sicily and Sardinia.[1] It is slightly larger than the state of Arizona in the United States. There are also two tiny sovereign nations within Italy: Vatican City and San Marino.

MOUNTAIN RANGES AND VOLCANOES

Italy's two major mountain chains, the Alps and the Apennines, cover about 40 percent of the country.[2] The Alps cut across the northern end of the country and are on both sides of Italy's borders with France, Austria, and Switzerland. The Alps have very high, rugged peaks with pyramid, pinnacle, rounded, and needlelike formations. Italy's highest point occurs in the Alps, on Mont Blanc at 15,577 feet (4,748 m).[3] However, the mountain rises to 15,781 feet (4,810 m) in France.[4] The Dolomites region of the Alps in northeastern Italy is known for its column-like limestone formations. Throughout the Italian Alps, there are long, thin lakes and valleys carved by glaciers thousands of years ago.

ITALY

SWITZERLAND
AUSTRIA
HUNGARY
SLOVENIA
CROATIA
BOSNIA AND HERZEGOVINA
Lake Maggiore
Lake Como
Lake Garda
Turin
Milan
Venice
Po River
Genoa
Florence
SAN MARINO
Pisa
Arno River
LIGURIAN SEA
Tiber River
ADRIATIC SEA
CORSICA (FRANCE)
Rome
VATICAN CITY
Bari
Naples
Vesuvius
Taranto
SARDINIA
Cagliari
TYRRHENIAN SEA
AEOLIAN ISLANDS
IONIAN SEA
Palermo
SICILY
Mount Etna
MEDITERRANEAN SEA
TUNISIA
N
W E
S
MALTA

KEY:
Capital
City
Point of Interest

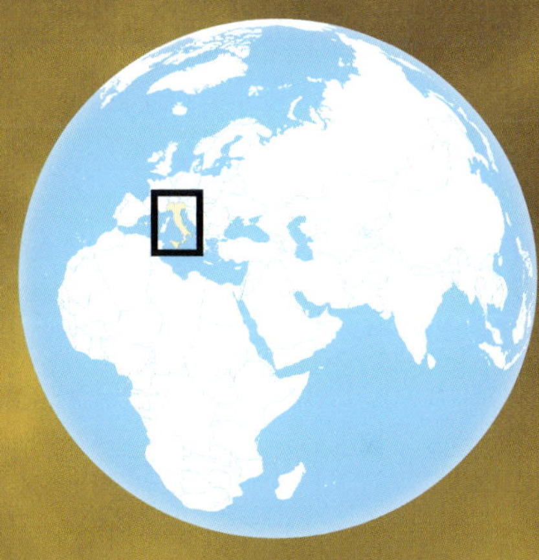

From the Alps, the Apennines run south down the entire length of Italy's peninsula and continue on the island of Sicily. Near central Italy, the mountain range widens to stretch across nearly the whole width of the Italian peninsula. The Apennines narrow again farther south. Northeast of Rome, a mountain called the Great Rock of Italy is the highest point in the Apennines at 9,554 feet (2,912 m).[5]

Italy is home to three main active volcanoes that have a recent history of eruption and are likely to erupt again. Vesuvius, located in southern Italy near the city of Naples, is the only active volcano in mainland Europe. Vesuvius famously erupted in 79 CE and buried the ancient towns of Pompeii and Herculaneum. Vesuvius is a stratovolcano, which means that its cone is made from layers of lava and ash from previous eruptions. It is part of a string of volcanoes formed on a boundary between Earth's tectonic plates. Vesuvius last erupted in 1944. However, it is considered one of the world's most dangerous volcanoes, as an eruption would endanger three million people who live near it.

Mount Etna is the tallest active volcano in Europe.

Located on the island of Sicily, Mount Etna is one of the largest volcanoes in the world, and it is also one of the world's most active volcanoes. The volcano erupted in February 2022, filling Sicily's sky with a brilliant light. Plumes of smoke rose from the volcano as lava flowed from its top.

Stromboli Volcano is Italy's third active volcano. It is located on an island of the same name off the northern coast of Sicily. Stromboli is one of the most active volcanoes globally and has been erupting regularly since 1932. However, its eruptions are generally smaller and less dangerous than

those of Vesuvius. Stromboli's explosions can be seen many miles away at sea, which has given it the nickname "The Lighthouse of the Mediterranean."

LAKES AND RIVERS

Italy's rivers are relatively short, with the longest, the Po, measuring only 400 miles (645 km) long.[7] The Po River begins in the Alps in northern Italy and flows east. It passes through cities such as Turin and Cremona and a very fertile valley, the Po Valley. The Po forms a large river delta where it meets and empties into the Adriatic Sea.

The Arno River flows from the Apennines in north-central Italy through the cities of Pisa and Florence. It empties on Italy's west coast into the Ligurian Sea. The Tiber River also originates in the Apennines. It flows south and passes through the city of Rome before it empties into the Tyrrhenian Sea.

Italy has about 1,500 freshwater lakes, many of which are in the north.[8] Many Italian lakes are small

Alpine lakes shaped by glaciers. Other lakes formed in the craters of extinct volcanoes. Some coastal lakes formed in prehistoric faults. Italy's largest and most famous lakes are found in valleys in the foothills of the Alps. These lakes include Lake Garda, Lake Maggiore, Lake Como, and Lake Lugano. These lakes are popular vacation spots with a mild climate and picturesque settings. Italy's largest lake, Lake Garda, has an area of 143 square miles (370 sq km).[9]

ITALY'S ISLANDS

A cluster of islands sits at the southern end of Italy's narrow peninsula. Italy has more than 400 islands. Many are tiny, less than 100 square miles (259 sq km), while a few are larger.[10] Sicily is the largest Italian island and covers an area of 9,830 square miles (25,460 sq km).[11] Its mountainous landscape includes Europe's highest active volcano, Mount Etna. Sicily is also home to a diverse array of plants and animals.

Found in the middle of the Mediterranean Sea, the island of Sardinia is slightly smaller than Sicily and is Italy's second-largest island. Its white sand beaches, blue waters, lagoons, and islets make it a popular vacation destination. The island is also home to Gola di Gorropu, Europe's largest canyon, and the Dunes of Piscinas, sand dunes that are 200 feet (61 m) tall.[12]

The island of Sardinia is famous for its beaches and crystal-clear waters. It is 120 miles (200 km) away from Italy's mainland.

Another popular vacation spot, the Aeolian Islands, sits north of Sicily. Volcanic activity formed the seven-island archipelago. Two of the islands, Vulcano and Stromboli, still have active volcanoes. All of the islands feature beautiful seascapes, historic villages, and delicious seafood.

PLAINS AND COASTAL REGIONS

The largest and most important Italian plain is the Padan Plain, also known as the Po Valley. Located between the Alps and the Apennines, the Po Valley covers more than 17,000 square miles (44,030 sq km) of Italy's 30,000 square miles (77,700 sq km) of plains. Most of the Po Valley sits between sea level and an altitude of 1,800 feet (550 m).[13] The Po River and several tributaries flow through the plain and provide important irrigation for crops and agriculture in the lower plain's fertile soil. Other significant plains in Italy include the Maremma of Tuscany and Lazio, the Pontine Marshes, the Campania Plain near Vesuvius, and the Apulian Plain. The Plain of Catania in Sicily is known for growing citrus fruits.

Italy's coastline along its mainland peninsula and islands extends 4,722 miles (7,600 km).[14] The coastline varies from high, rocky areas to

sandy beaches. One of the most famous rocky areas on the coast is Cinque Terre, located on Italy's northwest coast between Genoa and Pisa. On the coast from Tuscany to Campania, long, sandy beaches and higher, rockier sections can be found. Tall, rocky shores are broken up by spectacular white sand beaches along the Tyrrhenian Sea, especially in the south. Most of the Adriatic coast is flat, while the Po River delta is filled with lagoons. One of the most famous lagoons surrounds the city of Venice.

CLIMATE IN ITALY

Based on its geography, Italy lies in the temperate zone, which falls in Earth's middle latitudes between the tropics and polar regions. The country mainly experiences a Mediterranean climate, with hot, dry summers and cool, wet winters. Down its long peninsula, the climate in Italy's northern regions can vary significantly from that in its southern end. Italy's climate also varies by elevation. In the north, winters are cool and humid. On lower land, winter brings a lot of rain and fog to northern Italy. Summers in this region are not as hot as in southern Italy, and summer rains support farming and crops.

Farther south along the peninsula and on the Italian islands, summers are hot and dry, while winters are cool and rainy. Snow rarely falls in the winter, and summer temperatures can reach

> **From 1991 to 2020, the average summer temperature in Italy was 70.2 degrees Fahrenheit (21.2°C).[15]**

90 degrees Fahrenheit (32°C) or higher in July.[16] During the hot, dry summers, crops such as fruits and vegetables must be irrigated.

ITALY'S BIOMES

The Mediterranean forest, woodland, and scrub biome makes up most of Italy. It is sometimes called a chaparral biome. A biome is a community of plants and animals that adapt to and live in a specific climate. Around the world, there are five major biomes: aquatic, grassland, forest, desert, and tundra. These major biomes can be divided further into categories such as freshwater, marine, savanna, tropical rain forest, temperate rain forest, chaparral, and taiga.

The Mediterranean forest, woodland, and scrub biome is mainly found in mid-latitude regions within Mediterranean climate zones. These biomes typically experience hot, dry summers with cool, moist winters. Only five areas in the world have this type of biome, including the Mediterranean, south-central and southwestern Australia, and parts of Chile, California, and southern Africa. Although the Mediterranean forest, woodland, and scrub biome does not cover a lot of Earth's land, it holds extraordinary biodiversity. Many of its animal and plant species have adapted to live in long, hot summers with little rain.

CHAPTER THREE

PLANTS AND ANIMALS

taly is home to a rich diversity of plants and animals. The Italian land and climate create a variety of habitats that include mountains, coastal areas, forests, plains, and freshwater rivers and lakes. These habitats provide places for wildlife and plants to thrive throughout the country.

PLANTS AND VEGETATION

The World Resources Institute estimates that there are nearly 5,600 species of plants in Italy.[1] In the Alps, common plants and trees differ by elevation. Around the lakes in the Lombardy region, evergreen trees such as the cork oak, European olive, cypress, and

Every spring, poppies bloom in the fields of Tuscany. The flowers typically bloom from late April until mid-May.

The European olive is one of the most common trees in the Lombardy region.

cherry laurel are common. Larch and Norway spruce trees thrive at a little higher elevation on the mountain plains. In the highest altitudes in the Alps, pastures with grasses, sedges, and wildflowers grow. Mosses, lichens, and flags flourish at the mountain's snow line.

Most of the original forests and vegetation in the Po Valley have been cleared by humans over the centuries, and crops and pastures have replaced much of the indigenous plant life. Where there is enough water, poplar trees grow, while sedges grow in drier areas. In higher elevation areas of the plain, heather is common, along with forests of Scotch pine trees. However, the most common plants in the area are farmers' crops, such as wheat, corn, potatoes, rice, and sugar beets.

Farther south along the Italian peninsula and the Apennine region, Mediterranean vegetation is typical, including evergreens, holm oak, cork, juniper, bramble, laurel, myrtle, and dwarf palm.

Closer to the coast, olive, oleander, carob, Aleppo pine, and mastic trees grow. A scrub vegetation called maquis grows in areas where natural forests have been cleared. Maquis is mostly broad-leaf evergreen shrubs or small trees.

On Italy's farmlands, various fruits, herbs, vegetables, and plants thrive. Many of these plants are staples in Italian cuisine, which emphasizes fresh produce. Some common plants include olives, figs, grapes, and tomatoes.

ANIMALS

More than 57,000 animal species live in Italy's wide range of habitats. This represents more than one-third of the animals found in Europe.[2] However, over many centuries, humans have driven out much of the country's original animal life.

Ibex can be found around the Italian Alps. The wild goats tend to roam near the snow line throughout most of the year.

In the Alps and Apennines, there are animals that hibernate, such as the marmot, a species of large ground squirrel. Other mountain animals change the color of their fur based on the seasons as protection against predators. These animals include the Alpine rabbit and the rock partridge. Larger animals, including the ibex, chamois, and red deer, also live in the mountain regions. Other big mammals such as the lynx and brown bear are rare. In the Apennines, some species of foxes and wolves roam.

Birds and reptiles also live in Italy's mountain regions. Birds such as the black grouse, the golden eagle, and the wood grouse make their homes in Alpine habitats. The golden eagle is dark brown with golden feathers around its neck and head. The eagle's wingspan stretches almost eight feet (2.4 m).[5] Its large yellow feet have strong talons that it uses to grip prey. The Alpine salamander and newt also live in these mountainous regions.

In Italy's freshwater rivers and lakes, fish such as brown trout, sturgeon, and eel are common. In coastal waters, common species include the red mullet and the dentex. The dentex is a popular Italian seafood dish because of its rich flavor. White sharks, bluefin tuna, and swordfish swim on the southern coast. Italian bluefin tuna, packed in

olive oil, is considered some of the world's best canned tuna. In the warm waters off the southern coast, red coral and commercial sponges are common. Throughout the country, caves provide habitats for the greater horseshoe bat.

Italy has several endemic species, which are animals and plants that are unique to a geographic location. These species cannot be found naturally anywhere else in the world. Among the animals and plants found only in Italy are the Apennine chamois, spectacled salamander, Marsican brown bear, Calabrian black squirrel, Sicilian fir, and clouded Apollo butterfly.

THREATENED SPECIES

Many of Italy's plant and animal species face threats to their survival. Some species are being threatened by habitat loss and degradation. Habitats have been destroyed or damaged by growing cities and urbanization as well as farming and ranching. Habitats have also been harmed by climate change, air and water pollution, and the arrival of invasive species that compete with native species for resources.

In Italy, one threatened species is the Marsican brown bear, also known as the Apennine brown bear because it lives in the Apennines. Today, experts believe only about 50 of these bears remain in Italy. The male bear weighs as much as 440 pounds (200 kg) and can grow to a length of six feet, seven inches (2 m). The bear typically lives alone and will claim and roam a territory as large as 77 square miles (199 sq km).[6]

The Italian wolf is another threatened species that lives in the Apennine and western Alps mountain regions. A member of the gray wolf family, the Italian wolf typically weighs between 55 and 77 pounds (25–35 kg).[7] Its fur is a greyish-brown color. The wolf usually lives in a pack that consists of two to seven wolves. Over the years, the Italian wolf population has fluctuated. In the 1970s, an estimated 70 to 100 wolves remained in Italy. To preserve this species, Italy passed laws that protected the wolf from hunting. Since then, the wolf population has increased, with approximately 1,200 to 2,000 living in the Alps and Apennines.[8]

In 2022, approximately 149 animal species were listed by the IUCN as endangered and critically endangered.[10]

The Mediterranean monk seal is one of only two surviving species of monk seals in the world. Years of exploitation and harassment have left the species endangered and with a population of fewer than 700.[9] Before the Mediterranean monk seal was endangered, the seal was found throughout the Mediterranean waters, including Italy. A related species, the Caribbean monk seal, became extinct. Scientists are not sure of the exact date of the Caribbean monk seal's

The Mediterranean monk seal is an endangered species. Most of the surviving monk seals can be found off the coasts of Greece and Turkey. Some have been found near the coast of Italy.

permanent disappearance, but they believe some adult seals lived up until the 1960s or 1970s. The remaining Mediterranean monk seals live in only a few places, mainly in the Mediterranean and a few locations in the North Atlantic Ocean. The seals can weigh between 660 and 710 pounds

(299–322 kg) and grow to 7.9 feet (2.4 m) in length.[11] Males are black, while females are brown or grey. The seal has an average life span of 20 to 25 years.[12] Despite their endangered status, there is some hope. Conservation efforts have started to see results, with some seal populations increasing in size and monk seals appearing in places where they have not been spotted in decades, like in the coast of southern Italy.

CONSERVATION EFFORTS

The Italian government has worked to improve and protect the country's habitats and environment. Today, about 5 percent of Italy is protected national parkland.[13] The country's 24 national parks provide secure areas for animal and plant species. In addition, scientists can conduct research in the national parks to study the country's animal and plant species, learn about their relationships, habitats, and ecosystems, and assess their conservation status.

One example of a conservation effort is happening at Majella National Park. The park is located in central Italy near Abruzzo. At Majella, scientists are working to preserve plant biodiversity and

Visitors can go to Majella National Park and see the efforts scientists are making to conserve plant biodiversity. They can also appreciate the park's beautiful landscape, which includes waterfalls, canyons, and mountains.

protect rare plant species through botanical gardens, a seed bank, and a nursery.

On several of Italy's islands, another conservation project is working to restore the population of a species of seabird, the yelkouan shearwater. Invasive black rats on the islands caused havoc in seabird habitats. The rats hunted the birds' eggs and chicks, which caused a drastic decline in reproduction. Often, less than 10 percent of chicks survived.[14] The invasive rats lived on almost all islands where the yelkouan shearwater birds nested. As a result, the species population continued to decrease to the point where the International Union for the Conservation of Nature (IUCN) classified it as vulnerable.

Since 1999, conservationists have worked to remove the black rats from the Italian islands. Currently, there are seven rat-free islands, while removal is in process on several other islands. These efforts have yielded positive results. The percentage of yelkouan shearwaters that nest on rat-free islands has soared from 1 percent to almost 80 percent.[15]

HISTORY

Modern Italy has existed as an independent nation only since 1861. Yet the history of the people and societies that made the region their home goes back centuries. Each has contributed to modern Italian culture and society.

EARLY SOCIETIES

Some of the earliest evidence of humans living on the Italian peninsula comes from fossils that date back to 43,000 to 45,000 years ago.[1] Thousands of years later, more settlers traveled from Europe and Asia, crossing the Alps into the Po Valley around 1800 BCE. Later, these migrants divided into various groups and moved into central and southern Italy.

Italy is filled with famous historical monuments, such as the Roman Forum.

Evidence of the Etruscan civilization can be seen in decorated tombs.

The Etruscans emerged on the Italian peninsula around 800 BCE. They were skilled craftspeople and metalworkers who traded with the Greeks and later the Romans. The Etruscan civilization was a confederation of independent city-states that shared a common religion, language, and culture. A city-state is a region that is ruled by a major city. The people gathered together to celebrate and perform religious rites, which often involved animal sacrifices. The Etruscan tombs that survive today display wall paintings that show the Etruscan people dancing, making music, enjoying banquets, hunting, and fighting in battles. The Etruscans were praised as founders of cities and thrived on the Italian peninsula for centuries. In the 300s BCE, the Romans conquered the Etruscans, and they assimilated the Etruscans into the Roman Republic by 90 BCE. The Romans also adopted many parts of Etruscan culture, including certain clothing, religious practices, and architecture.

In the 800s and 700s BCE, ancient Greeks traveled to southern Italy and Sicily. They came for trade and to search for raw materials, particularly metals. They established permanent settlements as independent city-states in southern Italy. These communities brought many parts of Greek culture with them, such as writing and artistic styles, and shared these things with local communities, particularly the Etruscans.

RISE OF THE ROMAN EMPIRE

Legends say the city-state of Rome was founded around 753 BCE. However, historians are not exactly sure when Rome was formed. The earliest evidence shows a simple village that dates back as far as

Julius Caesar was instrumental in Rome's transition from a republic to a monarchy.

the 900s BCE. The settlement grew in the 600s and 500s BCE, and Latin people lived there. Architectural remains show that the Latin people traded with Greeks and Etruscans living on the peninsula. During this time, Rome was ruled by kings, and it steadily grew in size and wealth.

Around 509 BCE, Etruscan power declined, and Romans forced the last Etruscan king out of Rome. Rome became a republic ruled by the upper classes, which included senators and knights. In 451 BCE, Rome established the Twelve Tables, a code of laws for public, private, and political matters. By 338 BCE, the Roman Republic controlled the entire Italian peninsula. It also became a dominant maritime power in the Mediterranean Sea. In the early years of the republic, the Roman state grew quickly in size and military power because of its numerous wars and conquests. However, this led to years of political and social unrest.

Around 60 BCE, general Julius Caesar began his rise to power in the Roman Republic. In 46 BCE, Caesar became Rome's dictator. However, his rule did not last long. He was assassinated by political rivals in 44 BCE. After Caesar's assassination, Gaius Julius Caesar Octavianus, also known as Augustus Caesar or Octavian, replaced him and ruled Rome with another Roman politician, Mark Antony. When Antony died in 30 BCE, Octavian stood as the sole ruler of Rome. In 23 BCE, he became the first emperor of Rome, and Rome became known as the Roman Empire.

For two centuries, the Roman Empire experienced great peace and prosperity. The Romans built roads, bridges, and aqueducts throughout their land. By 117 CE, the Roman Empire expanded to its greatest point, controlling lands on three continents, including Asia, northern Africa, and most of Europe. It imposed Roman laws and customs on conquered lands.

JULIUS CAESAR

Julius Caesar was born in July of 100 BCE in the Roman Republic. Born into a noble family, Caesar became a notable general and politician. He became the governor of Gaul, a Roman province that included modern-day France and Belgium. For eight years in Gaul, from 58 to 50 BCE, Caesar strengthened his troops and military power.

When Caesar's political rivals in Rome demanded that he return to the city as a private citizen, Caesar had other plans. He marched his army from Gaul into Pompey, Italy, and Caesar emerged as the victor. He entered Rome and declared himself dictator in 46 BCE. As dictator, Caesar implemented social and political reforms, enlarged the senate, and decreased Rome's debt. Caesar also granted citizenship to foreigners living in the Roman Republic.

In 44 BCE, Caesar declared himself dictator for life. However, many senators became concerned about Caesar's increasing power and ambition. About a month after Caesar declared himself dictator for life, a group of senators betrayed and assassinated him.

Julius Caesar's assassination was so iconic that famed English playwright William Shakespeare wrote a play about it titled *The Tragedy of Julius Caesar.*

By the 200s CE, the Roman Empire was weakening as a result of instability and infighting. Emperor Constantine hoped to strengthen the empire by moving its center from Rome. In 324 CE, Constantine moved the empire's capital to the Greek colony of Byzantium, which is modern Istanbul, Turkey. He renamed the city Constantinople.

However, Constantine's efforts could not stop the empire's decline. When emperor Theodosius I died in 395 CE, the Roman Empire split into two parts. The western half was based in Rome, while the eastern half was based in Constantinople. Several groups of outsiders attacked the western empire, including the Vandals, the Huns, and the Visigoths. In 476 CE, the German chieftain Odoacer removed the last western Roman emperor, and the fall of Rome was permanent. The eastern empire, known as the Byzantine Empire, continued until the Turks conquered it in 1453 CE.

ITALIAN CITY-STATES

After the fall of the western Roman Empire, rival invaders and rulers fought for control of territory on the Italian peninsula between the 500s and the 1200s CE. Amid these battles, several Italian city-states emerged. The mountains and rivers across the Italian peninsula separated regions, making it easy for small city-states to grow independent of each other. Each city-state had its own government. Some city-states elected leaders, while ruling families led others. Sometimes, the city-states fought each other.

The Renaissance brought a massive influx of ideas, architecture, and art. Michelangelo's paintings on the ceiling of the Sistine Chapel are famous examples from this time period.

In the 1300s and 1400s, several significant city-states emerged on the Italian peninsula. These included the kingdoms of Sicily and Naples in the south, the Papal States in the central region, and three city-states called Florence, Milan, and Venice in the north. These large city-states became centers of trade, arts, and scientific advances. They exchanged goods and learning with the Byzantine empire and other civilizations.

THE RENAISSANCE

Starting around 1300, people began to have a renewed interest in classical Greek and Roman art, architecture, philosophy, literature, and science. This period between the 1300s and 1600s was called the Renaissance, which means "rebirth" in French. It sparked a movement called

Renaissance humanism, which revived interest in the study of the classical world. The key elements of humanism included an emphasis on the individual, an interest in non-religious studies, and an encouragement to ask the question, "What does it mean to be human?"

Italy's city-states and the wealthy families that ruled them, such as the Medicis of Florence and the Sforzas in Milan, became great benefactors of the arts and sciences. Their wealth allowed them to fund people such as architect Filippo Brunelleschi, scientist Galileo Galilei, and philosopher Niccolò Machiavelli.

During the Renaissance, artists, writers, and scholars in the Italian city-states created masterpieces of art, literature, and science. The Pope and wealthy families funded much of this work along with the construction of magnificent churches, palaces, and other public buildings. They decorated and filled these structures with art from renowned artists such as Leonardo da Vinci, Michelangelo, Sandro Botticelli, and Raphael.

Renaissance thinking, values, and arts moved up from southern Italy and then spread throughout the rest of Europe. Some of the significant accomplishments of this period include many famous works of art and literature, new ideas in philosophy, and discoveries in world exploration. Scientists developed theories about the solar system and the position of the sun. Astronomers discovered sunspots and new stars and changed the way people thought about the universe. The invention of a mechanized printing press accelerated the spread of Renaissance ideas and knowledge. These developments left a lasting mark on the world.

KINGDOM OF ITALY

Political unrest, economic hardship, and the bubonic plague spread through the peninsula in the 1600s and into the 1700s. In Italy and the rest of Europe, a privileged few were enormously wealthy, while most people lived in poverty. In the 1790s, France's Napoléon Bonaparte conquered Italy and brought ideas of nationalism, liberty, and equality to the country.

Napoléon Bonaparte, a French emperor, was proclaimed king of Italy in 1805.

After Napoléon's defeat in Belgium in 1815, most of the older rulers of the Italian states returned to power.

A movement to unify Italy emerged in the mid-1800s. Camillo Benso, count di Cavour united the country and established the Kingdom of Italy in 1861. He was Italy's first prime minister, and he named Emmanuel II as its monarch. In 1871, Italy added Venetia and the former Papal States, including Rome, into the kingdom.

WORLD WARS IN THE 1900s

The 1900s brought two world wars to Italy and countries across the globe. In 1914, the murder of Archduke Franz Ferdinand of Austria sparked a series of conflicts in Europe that sent the world's nations, including Italy, to war. In World War I (1914–1918), the Allies of the United Kingdom, France, Russia, Italy, Japan, and the United States fought against the Central powers of Germany, Austria-Hungary, and Turkey. At first, Italy was in an alliance with Germany and Austria-Hungary but remained neutral. In 1915, Italy joined the Allies. The war ended in 1918 with the defeat of the Central powers. However, Italy felt slighted in the resulting peace agreements. The country was not given territories that had been promised to it by the United Kingdom and France.

After the war, Italy fell into a time of severe economic depression and social unrest. This led to the rise of Benito Mussolini, who became Italy's prime minister in 1922. Mussolini established a fascist dictatorship in the country. The Italian king remained but only as a figurehead with no power. Instead, Mussolini became known as Il Duce, or "The Leader," and held all the power.

Mussolini wanted to create a new Roman empire and return Italy to its past dominance. He trained a large army and built up the country's military. In 1935, he invaded and conquered Ethiopia to increase Italy's colonial presence. Mussolini also became allies with Germany's new ruler, Adolf Hitler.

Peace across Europe, however, would not last for long. In 1939, Hitler sent German troops to invade Poland. The United Kingdom and France were Poland's allies and had promised to defend Poland. Within days, the United Kingdom and France declared war on Germany. World War II (1939–1945) had begun. More than 50 countries eventually joined the war. The United Kingdom, France, the United States, and the Soviet Union were among the countries fighting on one side as the Allied powers. Italy joined the Axis powers along with Germany and Japan.

However, failed attempts to conquer Greece and France, along with the Allied invasion of Sicily, led to the fall of Mussolini in 1943. Italy became divided, with the Allies controlling the south and the Germans holding the north. The Germans installed Mussolini as the head of the Italian Social Republic. As the war began to turn against Germany, German forces in Italy retreated. Italian partisans captured Mussolini and executed him in April 1945. In May of that year, German forces surrendered to the Allies in Europe. A few months later, in September, Japan surrendered in the Pacific, ending the war.

An estimated 457,000 Italian soldiers and civilians died during World War II.[3]

POSTWAR ITALY

After the war, Italy was left with its cities and economy in ruin. In 1946, the Italian people voted to end the monarchy and become a democratic republic. With help from other countries, including the United States, the country was able to restore its economy to prewar levels by the 1950s.

In 1952, Italy and five other countries founded the European Coal and Steel Community (ECSC), which eventually led to the creation of the European Union (EU). The EU is a political and economic alliance of European countries. The EU was formed to strengthen economic and political cooperation in Europe after World War II. It requires its members to follow specific laws about trade, security, immigration, and environmental regulations. Italy adopted the currency of the EU, the euro, in 2002.

In the 1990s, Italy was rocked by political scandals and corruption. In 1992, officials in Milan uncovered a series of bribery scandals. The investigation, called "Operation Clean Hands," led to many politicians, civil servants, and businessmen being arrested and sent to prison. Nearly all of Italy's political parties were involved in the corruption scandals. Most of the trials were broadcast on television for the public to follow. Many political parties dissolved in disgrace but were later remade under new names. Despite reform efforts, Italy is still plagued by corruption in business and politics.

CHAPTER FIVE

PEOPLE AND CULTURE

The Italian people and their culture have been influenced by their connection to the ancient civilizations on the peninsula. Thousands of years of traditions, customs, and heritage have created the Italy the world knows today.

ETHNIC GROUPS OF ITALY

Ethnic Italians make up 92 percent of the 61 million people living in Italy.[1] These people are descendants of the people who historically occupied the Italian peninsula, such as the Etruscans, Greeks, Germans, and Romans.

Italy's soccer team won the 2020 UEFA European Football Championship.

Italy is also home to many immigrants and their descendants. Since the 1970s, Italy has been a destination for immigrants seeking to make a home in western Europe. Many immigrants have arrived from Romania, Albania, China, India, Ukraine, and the Philippines. When several eastern European countries joined the EU in the early 2000s, immigration from eastern Europe increased. And as wars erupted in parts of the Middle East and North Africa, Italy has received hundreds of thousands of refugees from countries such as Morocco, Pakistan, and Egypt. Today, some of the largest non-Italian ethnic groups living in Italy include Romanians, Albanians, and the Maghreb from North Africa.

Over the years, many Italians have emigrated to other countries. Between 1876 and 1970, around 25 million Italians left the country searching for work and a better life.[2] Before the 1920s, many settled in North and South America. After World War II ended in 1945, numerous Italians moved to other countries in Europe, particularly France, Germany, and Switzerland.

REGIONAL DIFFERENCES

Italy was divided into separate city-states for much of its history. As a result, many Italians strongly identify with the culture of a particular city, town, or village. For example, a person from Tuscany would identify as a Tuscan, while a person from Sicily would say they are Sicilian. For many Italians, their local patriotism is stronger than their national identity.

There are also regional differences between northern and southern Italy, with the city of Rome marking the north-south divide of the country. Northern Italy industrialized in the late 1800s and

Sicilian culture differs from other cultures in Italy. Sicilian shops sometimes close between 1:00 p.m. and 4:00 p.m. so people can enjoy lunches with their families.

is viewed as being more modern, prosperous, and business minded. Some of Italy's largest cities, such as Rome, Venice, Milan, and Florence, are located in Italy's northern half. Cities in southern Italy, such as Bari, Matera, and Sorrento, are typically smaller and are associated with a slower pace of life and traditional family values.

LANGUAGE

Italian is the official language of Italy and is spoken by a large majority of the country's residents. The standard form of Italian is the one spoken in Tuscany, but there are many regional dialects around the country. Some regional dialects, such as those spoken on the islands of Sicily and

Sardinia, can be difficult for non-Italians and even some Italians from other regions to understand.

Other languages are also spoken in various regions of Italy. German is frequently spoken in some of the Alpine valleys in northern Italy. In Trentino–Alto Adige/Südtirol, the upper valley of the Adige River, German and Italian are both official languages. French is spoken in the Valle d'Aosta in northwest Italy and is a second official language. In southern Italy, groups of people speak Albanian, Croatian, and Greek. On the island of Sardinia, many people speak Sardinian.

RELIGION

Italy's history has long been entwined with the Roman Catholic Church. The head of the Roman Catholic Church, the pope, lives in Vatican City, which is an independent state located within Rome. For centuries, Vatican City has attracted many religious pilgrims to come and worship at

Saint Peter's Basilica, which is next to the Vatican Palace. People make pilgrimages to many other sacred sites and churches throughout Italy, including the town of Assisi, where Saint Francis, who is one of Italy's patron saints, was born. In 1929, Roman Catholicism was made the state religion under the Lateran Treaty.

Despite its long history with the Catholic Church, Italy gave up Catholicism as a state religion in 1985 to become a secular state. This decision ended mandatory religious teaching in public schools and reduced state payments to the church.

Today, more than 80 percent of Italians are Roman Catholics.[3] Italy is also home to a small number of Protestant Christians and Jehovah's Witnesses. There are also small Jewish communities scattered throughout the country, many of which survived Nazi persecution during World War II. A small number of people are Muslim, while other Italians are not affiliated with any organized religion. In Italy, freedom of religion is guaranteed by the country's constitution.

SCIENCE AND TECHNOLOGY

Throughout history, Italy has been home to many important scientists and scientific advances. In ancient times, the Romans demonstrated remarkable engineering and architectural skills in constructing aqueducts, bathhouses, and other public works that are still standing today. During the Renaissance, Italian astronomer and scientist Galileo Galilei supported the Copernican system, which correctly stated that Earth and other planets revolved around the sun. His work laid the foundation for scientists of the future.

Other Italian scientists invented the barometer, the electric battery, the process of electroplating, and the radiotelegraph. Today, many Italians are working in scientific research and development. The National Research Council, founded in 1923, is the country's principal research organization. It partners with private and university research centers to conduct scientific work on various subjects.

ART MASTERPIECES

Italy is known worldwide for its impressive art masterpieces. Some of the world's most famous artists, sculptors, and architects are Italian. These include Renaissance artists like Giotto, Donatello, Michelangelo, Leonardo da Vinci, Sandro Botticelli, and Giovanni Bellini.

Italy's artistic traditions can be traced to the Etruscans and the Greeks who lived on the peninsula. These civilizations created many works of art and built magnificent temples that still remain. The ancient Romans built architectural wonders, including outdoor theaters, temples, and public meeting places such as the Roman Forum and the Colosseum. Ancient Roman aqueducts still carry water to the city.

THE SISTINE CHAPEL

The Sistine Chapel in the Vatican Palace is famous for the frescoes Michelangelo painted on the chapel's ceiling and upper walls. The artist began painting the ceiling frescoes, which display scenes from the Bible's Old Testament, in 1508. Behind the altar, Michelangelo painted *The Last Judgment* from 1534 to 1541. Michelangelo's work in the Sistine Chapel is considered one of the greatest artistic achievements in Western history.

Dancer and painter Simona Atzori, who was born without arms, has performed at the Vatican as well as at the opening ceremony of the Paralympics in Turin, Italy, in 2006.

Italy's Renaissance birthed timeless pieces of art and architecture. Some of the most well-known Italian paintings from the period include Botticelli's *Birth of Venus*, Leonardo da Vinci's *Last Supper* and *Mona Lisa*, and Michelangelo's *The Creation of Adam* and *The Last Judgment*. Additionally, Michelangelo's *David* is the world's most famous sculpture.

Italy's creative arts continued after the Renaissance and into subsequent centuries. Today, the works of Italian artists such as sculptor Marino Marini continue to impress the country's visitors each year. And Italy's working artists, such as Arcangelo Sassolino and Maurizio Cattelan are primarily known for their sculptures and installations. They are adding to Italy's artistic traditions and creating new art for the world to enjoy.

MICHELANGELO

Michelangelo di Lodovico Buonarroti Simoni was an Italian painter, sculptor, and architect. He was born in 1475 in Caprese, Italy. Growing up in Florence, a city of great artists and sculptors, 13-year-old Michelangelo was apprenticed to a painter named Domenico Ghirlandaio. After a year with Ghirlandaio, Lorenzo de' Medici, the ruler of the city-state, took Michelangelo under his wing. With the expansive Medici art collection at his disposal, Michelangelo studied sculpting.

Over the years, Michelangelo created many masterpieces including marble sculptures like the *Pietà* and *David*. He also painted the ceiling and west wall of the Sistine Chapel for the pope, spending hours at a time on his back to paint. Later in his life, Michelangelo also turned to architecture. He designed the Medici Chapel and was named the chief architect of Saint Peter's Basilica in 1546. In 1564, Michelangelo died at 88 years old, leaving the world with countless pieces of art that would awe the world even hundreds of years later.

Michelangelo was one of the most famous artists of the Renaissance.

MUSIC

Music has long been an important part of Italian life. The Gregorian chant, the madrigal, and troubadour songs were all forms of early Italian music. Notable Italian composers include Antonio Vivaldi, Giovanni Pierluigi da Palestrina, and Alessandro Scarlatti.

Opera was developed in Italy in the late 1500s, and for many years, Italy remained the center of the European opera world. Giacomo Puccini is considered the founding father of Italian opera and composed several famous operas, including *Madama Butterfly*, *Tosca*, and *La Bohème*. In the 1800s, Giuseppe Verdi was a giant in the Italian opera world, and his operas were extremely popular and performed worldwide. His *La traviata* is the world's most-performed opera.[4]

In the 1900s, Italian musicians including violinist Uto Ughi and pianist Maurizio Pollini entertained the world. Singers Luciano Pavarotti, Andrea Bocelli, and Cecilia Bartoli thrilled audiences with their talent. Singer and songwriter Laura Pausini is a

ITALIAN FASHION

Italy is known worldwide for its designers and high fashion. The Italian fashion industry is based in Milan. The world's finest models, designers, and photographers travel to Milan to work with famous Italian fashion houses, such as Versace, Gucci, Miu Miu, Valentino, Prada, Dolce & Gabbana, Armani, and more. Twice a year, the city of Milan hosts Milan Fashion Week. Established in 1958, the event presents about 70 fashion shows via catwalk shows, designer showrooms, and other exhibitions.[5] The event's goal is to promote Italian fashion designers in Italy and internationally.

five-time Grammy Award winner for her music. And in Milan, La Scala remains one of the world's premier opera houses.

SPORTS

Soccer is Italy's most popular sport. More than 4.3 million Italians play soccer each year.[6] Italy's national soccer association was formed in 1898 and is part of the Union of European Football Associations. Italy's national teams typically wear a blue uniform with a crest featuring Italy's flag colors and championship stars. Because of the blue uniforms, the men's team's nickname is the Azzurri and the women's team is called the Azzurre, which both mean "the Blues."

In addition to the national teams, many Italian cities also have a professional club that plays in one of three divisions. The most dominant club in the men's top professional soccer league is Juventus from Turin. At the start of the 2022 season, Juventus had won 67 national and international titles.[7]

> In 2006, Italy's men's national soccer team won its fourth World Cup title, which was second only to Brazil's five titles.[8]

Along with soccer, sports such as bicycle racing, automobile racing, motorcycle racing, basketball, boxing, tennis, and downhill skiing are also popular among Italians. Bocce, a bowling game played on clay courts, is also commonly played in Italy.

FOOD

Food is an integral part of the Italian lifestyle. Distinct but simple ingredients such as tomato, cheese, garlic, olive oil, and cured meat are everyday staples in many dishes. Sharing these dishes with family and friends is an essential aspect of the Italian food culture.

Pasta is one of Italy's most iconic foods. From ravioli in the Lombardy region to lasagna and tortellini in Bologna, cannelloni in Sicily, and spaghetti with tomato sauce in Naples, pasta is an important part of Italian cuisine. Pasta is generally served with a sauce. The type of sauce varies by region and by the availability of local ingredients. The dish may include meats, seafood, or vegetables.

Ragù alla Bolognese is the national dish of Italy and is immensely popular worldwide. The pasta dish features a meat-based sauce made from pork, beef, or veal and onions, carrots, pancetta, and butter. The dish originated near Bologna, Italy, which gave the dish its name.

HISTORY OF PIZZA

The first record of pizza dates back to 997 CE, when it was a stuffed bread folded and cooked in the oven. Fillings typically included lard, garlic, salt, olive oil, cheese, and herbs. Between 1700 and 1800, pizza became linked to the city of Naples. For people in Naples, pizza was a cheap food that was nutritious and easy to make. Street vendors sold pizza in stalls. In the 1700s tomatoes first arrived in Italy, and the traditional Neapolitan pizza was first created. This was made with garlic, olive oil, tomato, and oregano. When Neapolitan immigrants traveled to the United States in the 1900s, they brought the tradition of pizza with them.

One of Italy's traditions is the *aperitivo*, a light predinner drink that typically takes place between 6:00 p.m. and 8:00 p.m. The aperitivo is meant to give people an appetite for dinner, which is usually between 8:00 p.m. to 10:00 p.m. Italians usually pair a low-alcohol drink with snacks such as mozzarella balls, mini-crostini, and olives.

MAJOR HOLIDAYS AND FESTIVALS

Italians celebrate Christian holidays, such as Christmas and Easter, along with New Year's Day on January 1 and Labor Day on May 1. The national holiday of Liberation Day is on April 25. It marks the fall of Mussolini's regime and the end of the Nazi occupation of Italy in 1945.

Across Italy, religious holidays often feature many colorful traditions. For example, in Florence on Easter Sunday, a tradition called Scoppio del Carro, or the "Explosion of the Cart," occurs. In a tradition that dates back hundreds of years, an elaborately decorated wagon is pulled through the streets of Florence by a pair of oxen in a procession. The wagon carries a flame lit by a priest and delivers it to the archbishop of Florence at the Duomo, the city's main cathedral. After the oxen have been detached from the cart and moved to a safe distance, the archbishop uses the flame to light a small rocket. The rocket flies down a wire outside the church and collides with the cart, which is loaded with fireworks. The collision causes the cart to "explode" in a fireworks display. For many towns and villages, the feast of the local patron saint is another major holiday. Celebrations often include fireworks, processions down city streets, marching bands, costumes, food, and special markets.

Festivals are also common across Italy throughout the year. One of the largest religious festivals is Carnevale, which occurs right before Lent, the solemn six-week period before Easter. Towns throw parades and masquerade balls. There are street performances, concerts, and boat parades. Pranks are also common during this time, which leads to the Italian saying, *a Carnevale ogni scherzo vale*, which translates to "anything goes at Carnival."

Italy's long history in agriculture can be seen in various festivals that celebrate the harvest, food, and fishing. Often, these festivals reflect a region's traditional culture. For example, in Spello, the Olive and Bruschetta Festival celebrates the end of the olive harvest. In Canelli, a hazelnut festival celebrates the important local crop, while the people of Termoli, a town on the Adriatic coast, celebrate the town's fishing traditions in a fish festival.

Scoppio del Carro is one of Italy's most colorful annual traditions.

CHAPTER SIX

POLITICS

taly and its people have been ruled by kings, emperors, and dictators throughout its history. By the end of World War II, Italy was in disarray, and the Italian people were ready for a new form of government, one that would give them more of a voice. In 1946, Italians voted to end the constitutional monarchy and establish a republic. At the same time, an elected assembly began to draft a new constitution, which was approved in 1948.

Today, the Italian government is made up of three branches. The legislative branch includes Parliament, which debates and passes laws. The executive branch carries out the laws and manages the government, and the judicial branch enforces the laws.

The president of Italy resides in the Quirinal Palace in Rome. The Quirinal is the tenth-largest palace by area in the world.

A PARLIAMENTARY REPUBLIC

Italy is a parliamentary republic. Executive power resides with the Council of Ministers, led by the president of the council, also known as the prime minister. The ministers execute laws and make other political decisions. They do this by presenting bills to Parliament or by passing decrees. The prime minister is typically a member of the political party that holds the most seats in Parliament. Italy's president appoints the prime minister with Parliament's approval. Parliament can dismiss the prime minister at any time.

The president is Italy's head of state and part of the executive branch. The president is elected by an electoral college, which includes members of Parliament and regional representatives. The president serves a seven-year term. Presidential duties include representing Italy on formal occasions such as the signing of treaties. The president also calls for elections, calls for referendums, and officially puts laws passed by Parliament into effect. In Italy, only two presidents, Giorgio Napolitano in 2013 and Sergio Mattarella in 2022, have been elected to a second term.

ITALY'S CONSTITUTION

Italy's constitution is a set of 139 articles that establish the country's basic rules of society. The articles can be divided into three main categories: fundamental principles, citizen rights and duties, and organization of the Republic. The writers of Italy's constitution intentionally made it very difficult to amend it. This was done to prevent potential dictators from making changes that would give them too much power. Since 1948, only 13 amendments have been made.

PARLIAMENT

A bicameral Parliament passes Italy's laws. It is made up of two chambers, the Chamber of Deputies and the Senate. The Italian people elect the 630 members of the Chamber of Deputies, the lower house, through a proportional representation system. In this electoral system, political parties gain seats in proportion to the number of votes they receive. All Italian citizens aged 18 or older may vote.

In the Senate, 315 members are elected by the Italian people via a proportional representation system. Additional senators, who are not elected, can be appointed. For example, former presidents of the republic become senators for life, and the president may appoint additional life senators. Members of the Chamber of Deputies and the Senate are elected for five-year terms. Members of both houses of Parliament have immunity from arrest,

Sergio Mattarella was elected president in January 2015.

Italy's Chamber of Deputies meets at Palazzo Montecitorio, which is in Rome.

criminal trial, and search while they are in office. However, Parliament can vote to strip ministers of their immunity.

The most important duty of Parliament is to pass legislation. Bills can be proposed in Parliament by the government, individual members, regional councils, or petitioning citizens. After a bill is proposed, it needs to gain the approval of the Chamber of Deputies and the Senate. Both houses review and discuss the bill. The bill typically shuffles between the two houses as they each make amendments. The bill is officially approved once both houses agree on the same text.

After the two houses of Parliament approve the bill, it is promulgated, or formally declared, by the president. If the president opposes the bill, the bill can be sent back to Parliament for further debate. If the bill passes a second time, the president must promulgate it. The law becomes effective when published in the *Gazzetta Ufficiale*, the official journal of record for the Italian government.

REGIONAL GOVERNMENT

Italy is divided into 20 regions, each with its own government. The Italian constitution gives the regions some freedom in making local decisions. Many are governed by regional councils elected by the people and have the power to pass laws and issue regulations.

The regions are further divided into 107 provinces for local governments, which are then divided again into several thousand communes, which is Italy's smallest government unit. Councils, committees, and mayors run communes. They have the authority to collect local taxes, operate the police force, issue ordinances, and run certain public health services. They are also responsible for local services such as public transportation, garbage collection, and street lighting.

Five regions, Valle d'Aosta, Friuli–Venezia Giulia, Sardinia, Sicily, and Trentino–Alto Adige/Südtirol, have special status, which gives their governments additional constitutional powers and more control over local laws and money. These regions were granted special status to preserve their cultural and linguistic differences.

JUDICIAL SYSTEM

In Italy, the judicial system is independent of the legislative and executive branches of government, as stated by the constitution. The judiciary implements the laws passed by Parliament. The judicial system is made up of a series of courts and a body of judges. Typically, judges are recruited through an exam given by the Minister of Justice. Those who pass the exam are assigned to courts depending on competence. However, there are some exceptions to this procedure. For example, judges of the Constitutional Court are appointed by the president, Parliament, and other courts.

The judicial system is unified, which means that every court is part of a national network. Minor legal matters are heard by conciliators, who are like mediators. Courts of first instance are the first step in the legal process and hear civil cases and some criminal cases within their jurisdiction.

The Supreme Court of Cassation building overlooks the Tiber River.

Minor cases may be presided over by a single judge, while a panel of judges may preside over more serious cases. The court of assizes hears serious criminal cases such as those involving murder or terrorism. Courts of appeal review the judgments made by the courts of first instance and courts of assizes.

The highest court in the country is the Supreme Court of Cassation. It reviews judgments from the courts of appeal. It focuses only on the application of law and not the facts of

the case. The Constitutional Court is made up of 15 judges and hears cases involving disputes over constitutional matters. Both the Supreme Court of Cassation and the Constitutional Court are in Rome.

POLITICAL PARTIES

Italy has many political parties, and some are active only in certain regions. The country's multiparty system makes it unlikely that any single party will gain a majority of seats in Parliament. Therefore, coalitions between several parties are often formed to create majorities.

After World War II, two main political parties, the centrist Christian Democratic Party and the left-wing Italian Communist Party, dominated the country for several decades. During this time, several smaller political parties also had influence, such as the Italian Socialist Party. Then in the 1990s, the collapse of communist regimes in Europe shook Italian politics. And in 1992, investigations discovered widespread corruption in the Italian government, and many senior government officials were arrested or resigned. The reputations of the main political parties were severely damaged, and many political parties broke apart.

In the aftermath of the scandal, the Italian Communist Party became the Democratic Party of the Left and eventually today's Democratic Party. Meanwhile, the Christian Democratic Party faded. Today, Italy's four main political parties are the Democratic Party, Northern League, Forza Italia, and Five Star Movement. Other significant parties include the far-right Brothers of Italy, the center-right Popular Alternative, the Liberal Popular Alliance–Italian Republican Party, and Us with Italy.

NATO

NATO is a multinational military alliance founded in 1949. It consists of 30 member countries, including Italy and the United States. NATO has conducted operations in Afghanistan, Iraq, Kosovo, and Somalia. It also worked to deter aggression from Russia, particularly in eastern Europe. Article 5 of the NATO treaty says, "An armed attack against one or more [member states] in Europe or North America shall be considered an attack against them all."[1]

FOREIGN POLICY

After World War II, Italy joined several multinational alliances to work toward the country's stability and security. In 1949, Italy became one of the original members of the North Atlantic Treaty Organization (NATO), an alliance of nations with the goal of providing security and stability for its members. Italy also joined the European Coal and Steel Community, an organization that sought to standardize European regulation of those industries, in 1952. In 1957, Italy became a founding member of the European Economic Community (EEC), which aimed to promote economic cooperation among its members. In 1993, the

EEC was replaced by the European Union (EU). The EU is a coalition of 27 European countries, including Italy, with the goal of eliminating trade, economic, and social barriers among member countries. The EU's headquarters are located in Brussels, Belgium.

ITALIAN ARMED FORCES

Italy's military is one of Europe's most powerful armed forces. It includes the Italian Army, the Italian Navy, the Italian Air Force, and the Carabinieri. The Carabinieri operates as the country's military police and can also be sent on missions abroad as a combat force. In 2021, there were about 170,000 active members of the Italian armed forces.[2] All Italian soldiers are volunteers, as Italy's mandatory military service was abolished in 2004.

The main focus of Italian military operations involves ensuring foreign and domestic national security and participating in NATO and other coalition military operations worldwide. In early 2022, Italy had more than 9,000 troops deployed on 34 missions in 21 countries.[3]

On May 4, 2022, the Italian army celebrated the 161st anniversary of its founding.

CHAPTER SEVEN

ECONOMICS

After World War II, the Italian economy, which was based mainly on agriculture, was in shambles. In the following years, the Italian government focused on rebuilding the country's economy and pursued industrialization. In a few decades, Italy transformed itself from a country that relied mainly on agriculture to one of the world's most industrialized economies. A large part of the Italian economy is driven by small and midsize businesses that manufacture high-quality consumer goods such as jewelry, leather, clothing, furniture, shoes, and more.

In 2020, Italy's gross domestic product (GDP) totaled $2.49 trillion.[1] GDP is the total amount of income generated from the sale of final goods and services

The Bank of Italy is the country's central bank.

in a country. It measures the economic strength of a nation. When measured by GDP, Italy is the 12th-largest national economy in the world.[2]

CURRENCY

The official currency of Italy is the euro. Italy is a member of the eurozone, a group of countries in the EU that use the euro as their official currency. Vatican City also uses the euro as its currency.

The euro replaced the Italian lira, the country's previous currency, in 2002. The European Central Bank issues the euro, the second-most-traded currency on the world's foreign exchange markets after the US dollar. The euro is also a major global reserve currency. A global reserve currency is held in large amounts by central banks or other monetary authorities of foreign countries as part of their reserves. It can be used in international transactions and investments and is often considered a safe and stable currency.

MAJOR INDUSTRIES

Italy's economy relies heavily on services and manufacturing. Services accounted for nearly 67 percent of the country's total GDP in 2020 and employed about 70 percent of Italy's total labor force.[3] Banking and financial services are an important part of Italy's services sector, with multinational banks, insurance companies, and other credit industries contributing to the economy. Wholesale and retail sales, telecommunications, business services, and education are also parts of Italy's services sector.

Tourism is an integral part of Italy's economy and services sector. Millions of tourists visit Italy each year to see sights such as Rome's Colosseum, the Florence Cathedral, the Grand Canal in Venice, the Leaning Tower of Pisa, Saint Peter's Basilica in Vatican City, and Florence's Uffizi Gallery. Vacationers travel to Italy's beautiful lakes, ski resorts, and Mediterranean coastal villages. The tourism industry also employs many people in restaurants, hotels, shops, and transportation. In 2019, nearly 100 million tourists visited Italy.[4] Those numbers significantly dropped in 2020 because of the COVID-19 pandemic but rebounded in 2022.

Industry, including manufacturing, is also an essential part of the Italian economy. Industry contributed about 22 percent to Italy's GDP in 2020.[5] Italy produces many high-quality specialty goods. The industrial sector includes many family-owned small to midsize businesses. Companies create finely crafted ceramic tiles, wooden furniture, textiles, jewelry, footwear, appliances, clothing, and more. Chemical and food and beverage manufacturers are spread throughout the country. Other industries include iron and steel, naval ship construction, machinery, and aerospace.

AGRICULTURE

Once a dominant part of Italy's economy, agriculture contributed about 2 percent to GDP in 2020 and employed about 3.6 percent of the country's labor force.[6] Today, about 36 percent of Italy's land is used for agriculture.[7] Many farms are located in the southern regions of Italy, and nearly all are family operated. Italy's Mediterranean climate and fertile soil make it an ideal place to grow grapes. Italy's vineyards create some of the world's best wines. In 2020, Italy was the world's leading producer of wines. It is also a leading global grower of numerous fruits, including oranges, peaches, olives, apples, and apricots. Italy's agriculture sector also includes robust fishing and livestock industries.

EXPORTS AND IMPORTS

Italy is one of the world's largest exporters of goods to other countries. Because Italy's manufacturing sector produces many first-rate goods, the country is an important producer of luxury goods for the global market. The country exports clothing and footwear from some of

Some farms grow plants hydroponically, which means the plants don't need soil to grow.

the world's most famous fashion brands. Other main exports include machinery and mechanical equipment, electronic equipment, pharmaceutical products, and motor vehicles, including luxury vehicles. Italy's main export partners are Germany, the United States, and France.

Italy has the second-highest industrial production output in Europe after Germany.[8]

Italy exports luxury vehicles such as Ferraris.

Italy lacks natural energy resources, which makes it dependent on foreign energy. As a result, Italy's main imports are fuels, with oil coming from North Africa and the Middle East and natural gas coming from Russia and other countries. Other significant imports include machinery and raw materials. Italy also imports food because its land is not suitable for growing all of the crops and foods its people need. Many of Italy's non-fuel imports come from EU countries.

Overall, Italy exports more goods and services than it imports. In 2020, Italy exported $555 billion in goods and services, while it imported $485 billion in foreign goods and services.[9] Because it exports more goods and services than it imports, Italy has a positive trade balance. Generally, a positive trade balance can lead to economic growth and create more jobs, and it is usually viewed as a sign of economic strength.

NATURAL RESOURCES

Italy is one of the world's leading producers of pumice, pozzolana, and feldspar. Pumice is a light and porous volcanic rock that forms when frothy, glassy lava solidifies quickly. It is used as an abrasive in cleaning compounds and incorporated into poured concrete, insulation, tile, and plaster. Pozzolana is a type of cement made by grinding a volcanic material with powdered hydrated lime. Feldspar is a group of minerals found in many of Earth's rocks. It is used in many products such as drinking glasses, fiberglass, floor tiles, and tableware.

Marble is another resource that Italy is famous for. Marble can be extracted from different places in Italy, from Sicily in the south to the Alps in the north. The Apuan Alps, a mountain range in northern Tuscany, produce Italy's world-famous white marble, Carrara marble. This material has been used for iconic buildings and art, including the Pantheon in Rome and Michelangelo's

There are many marble quarries in the region near Carrara.

statue *David*. Other regions of Italy, such as Lazio, Sicily, Verona-Vincenza, the Po Valley, Lombardy, Venice, and Puglia, produce colored marble.

TRANSPORTATION

Italy has a well-developed transportation system. The Italian railroad links cities throughout the country and neighboring nations. The Italian government owns and operates about 80 percent of the country's rail system.[10] Rail lines run along both coasts and across the Italian peninsula. Other rail lines run across the Alps from Italy to France, Austria, and Slovenia. The Simplon Tunnel is one of the world's longest railroad tunnels at 12.5 miles (20 km) and connects Italy and Switzerland.[11]

Italy boasts 303,043 miles (487,700 km) of paved roadways.[12] The country has one of Europe's highest rates of automobile ownership, with 80 percent of residents owning a car in 2021.[13] To handle all those drivers, Italy's highway system is one of the world's best, with expressways to carry heavy traffic along popular routes. A major highway connects France and Italy through the Mont Blanc Tunnel.

Italy's extensive coastline features many ports where ships carry imports and exports by sea. Major seaports include Augusta, Cagliari, Genoa, Livorno, Taranto, Trieste, and Venice. The country also has about 1,491 miles (2,400 km) of inland waterways used for transportation.[14] These waterways are located mainly in the north and include the Po River, the Italian lakes, and a network of Venetian and Po River Valley canals. Ferries carry freight and passengers between Italy's islands and the mainland.

A small amount of cargo is transported by air and is handled by main airports near Milan and Rome. International airports for passengers are located in Venice, Rome, and Milan. In addition, many regional airports are scattered throughout the country.

TRAVELING IN THE EUROPEAN UNION

EU citizens can travel throughout the countries of the EU without having to show a passport or visa. They do not have to pay roaming charges on their mobile phones while traveling, and their credit card transactions aren't charged additional fees for being in a different country. Driving is not a problem, as a driver's license from one EU country is valid throughout the EU. EU citizens can also study and work in all EU countries.

ITALY TODAY

Officially forming in 1861, Italy has transformed from a traditional agricultural society to a modern, industrialized nation. Although the country is unified under a national government, the country's various regions maintain strong cultural identities. These differences make Italy a culturally rich and diverse community for people of all backgrounds.

DAILY LIFE IN ITALY

Daily life in Italy is fairly similar to that in other European countries or in the United States. Teens go to school, hang out with friends, listen to music, go to the

Each of Italy's regions has a distinct culture and characteristic. Venice is known for its canals and beautiful architecture.

movies, play video games, and shop for the latest fashions. They text, make videos, and post on social media with smartphones.

Most Italian families live in apartments or condominiums in large cities. Within cities, the apartments and condominiums are often created in old *palazzi storici*, which are historical buildings with beautiful architecture that have been converted into multifamily housing units. In suburbs, apartments are more likely to be built in modern towers. Many apartments and condominiums have balconies that provide a small outdoor space for residents. Italians typically use their balconies for various activities such as dining, washing clothes, and hanging clotheslines. Balconies can also serve as outdoor gardens or places for extra storage. Wealthy Italians may afford an expensive *villetta*, a small, detached home, in the suburbs. Many middle-class Italians living in large cities also own summer homes in the country, by the coast, or in the mountains.

In more rural areas outside of the major cities, the average family lives in a two-story home. Each region has its own style of traditional home. On the island of Sardinia, a *stazzo* is a rectangular house made of granite blocks that has one or two rooms. There is often an oven or small storage room outside the main house. In Apulia, the trulli are cone-shaped buildings built with dry stone. They have few windows and keep residents warm in the winter and cool in the summer. Near Salento, the *masserie* are former farmhouses, many of which have been converted into bed-and-breakfast inns or rustic homes. The typical home in Sicily, the *baglio*, is a farm with a large courtyard. Many have multiple buildings that served as houses, stables, and warehouses. Many bagli have been renovated and are now used for tourism. *Baite* in the mountains are alpine cabins with sloping roofs made of stone and wood. And the *cascine* is a large farmhouse often on an agricultural estate in the Italian countryside.

EDUCATION IN ITALY

In Italy, school is mandatory for all children ages six to 16. Public schools are free and open to all residents of Italy. Most schools and universities across Italy are operated by the state and use uniform programs of studies across the country. Private schools, often run by religious groups, are also allowed, although a small number of Italian students attend them. Children attend kindergarten between the ages of three and six. Beginning at age six, children attend primary school. At age 11, they move up to secondary school for eight years, which has two phases: lower secondary school and upper secondary school.

After secondary school, students can choose to attend a variety of technical and trade schools, art schools, teaching schools, and other postsecondary prep schools. Some choose to continue their education further by attending a university. University admission is unrestricted for most students who have earned a secondary school diploma. To receive a bachelor's degree, or *Laurea*, students typically study for three years. If they wish to continue their studies, students can study for two years to get their master's degree, or *Laurea magistrale*. A doctorate usually takes about three to four years to obtain, depending on the university and course of study.

> **Founded in about 1200, the University of Bologna is Italy's oldest university and one of the oldest in the world.[1]**

HOBBIES AND RECREATION

People in Italy enjoy several traditional leisure activities such as watching television, listening to the radio, reading newspapers, and going to the movies. Meeting with friends in public spaces remains an important part of Italian life. Young people meet up with friends daily, often in the city piazzas. They visit movie theaters, pizzerias, and dance clubs with friends.

Sports and outdoor activities are also popular among Italians. Millions of people cheer for the country's professional soccer clubs. Basketball has also grown in popularity after being introduced in Italy by the United States. Most Italian cities have a professional basketball team that plays in one of the country's leagues. Motor racing is also popular with grand prix tracks at Monza, where the Italian Grand Prix is held, and Imola, where the Emilia Romagna Grand Prix is run. Cycling races draw crowds of fans. The annual Giro d'Italia is a multistage cycling race usually held in May that attracts international cyclists each year.

Many Italians enjoy winter sports such as skiing and snowboarding in the Alps and other mountain ranges. The Italian mountains are also popular for summer hiking and climbing adventures. The rolling hills of Tuscany and Umbria provide an excellent landscape for less intense walking and mountain biking.

The Italian government imposed strict lockdowns and sanitizing operations in public areas as COVID-19 cases rose.

Italy's extensive coastline offers many water sports and activities, such as sailing and windsurfing. Scuba diving is popular in Sicily and on some of Italy's smaller islands. Italians also enjoy recreation on the country's many lakes. River canoeing, rafting, and canyoning, which is a combination of hiking, climbing, and swimming through a canyon or gorge, are a few popular outdoor activities.

CHALLENGES AND CONCERNS

Like every nation in the world, Italy has challenges to face today and in the future. One of the biggest in recent years has been the COVID-19 pandemic that emerged in late 2019. Italy was one of the first European countries affected by the virus, and it quickly became an epicenter. The outbreak began in the Lombardy region in the north but spread throughout the country. Within weeks, hospitals were overwhelmed with sick and dying patients. To slow the spread of the virus, the Italian government issued a series of decrees that gradually increased restrictions and lockdowns in the northern regions hardest hit by the virus. Eventually, these lockdown decrees were expanded and applied to the entire country.

As other countries saw what was happening in Italy, they instituted lockdowns for citizens and closed businesses, schools, and borders to varying degrees. As the pandemic stretched into 2022, the lingering effects of these public health measures became apparent, from damage to the Italian economy to increasing mental health problems. However, the development of vaccines for the virus that causes COVID-19 helped Italy and the rest of the world slowly recover. Moving forward,

Italy continued to deal with COVID-19 as new variants emerged and scientists learned more about the disease.

Immigration is another challenge facing Italy. In 2020, Italy received about 40 percent of Europe's refugees and asylum seekers.[2] Although overall immigration has declined in recent years, the number of migrants attempting to reach Italy by sea has increased. The country's location in the Mediterranean has made it a destination for migrants who arrive in the country daily by boat from northern Africa and the Middle East. Many people in Italy are calling for stronger border enforcement, the deportation of migrants already in the country, and strengthening Italy's asylum rules. Those supporting anti-immigration policies argue that immigrants strain the economy when the country is forced to support basic needs such as housing and medical care. Giorgia Meloni and her popular far right-wing party Fratelli d'Italia ("Brothers of Italy") frequently linked the spread of COVID-19 with undocumented immigration. Although there is no concrete evidence for this

Many migrants and refugees arrive in Italy by boat. According to Amnesty International, many migrants are subject to exploitative work conditions and hate crimes motivated by racism.

belief, it is a view held by many Italians, especially after the COVID-19 pandemic decimated Italy's economy. Others, however, point out that Italy's future is being threatened by a declining birth rate. The country's population continues to age, with fewer babies being born and people living longer. They argue that immigration is a way to maintain the country's workforce and offset its aging population.

In 2021, Italy faced its worst recession since World War II. The economic problems caused by the pandemic worsened an economy already dealing with high youth unemployment and high levels of corruption. In 2020, lockdowns and restrictions shut down businesses and slowed the country's economic activity throughout the year, leaving many people unemployed.

Russia's invasion of Ukraine on February 24, 2022, also added to Italy's economic crisis. To show disapproval of the invasion, many countries in the EU, including Italy, decided to reduce Russian gas imports. But because Russia supplied 40 percent of Italy's natural gas, many Italians had to deal with increased gas prices.[4] Based on a survey

AGING POPULATION

Italy has the world's third-oldest population, after Japan and Monaco. In 2020, 23 percent of Italian people were aged 65 years or older. The average age in Italy is 45.7 years and is projected to grow older in future decades because people are living longer and there is a declining birth rate.[5] As the population ages, the economy will be impacted. Studies show that when population growth stops, GDP growth also slows. As the government needs to spend more money for health care and pensions, younger people will have to pay more to support the growing elderly population.

in April 2022, rising prices of goods and Russia's war with Ukraine were Italian consumers' top concerns. The COVID-19 pandemic, unemployment, and climate change were among the next most significant concerns.

LOOKING TO THE FUTURE

Once the center of the Roman Empire, Italy has transformed itself into a modern, industrialized nation. Yet it still cherishes its rich history and culture, developed over centuries from the people and civilizations who lived on the Italian peninsula. Today, Italy is home to countless artistic, historical, and cultural treasures that draw visitors from around the world. As Italy successfully balances its past and present, the future looks bright for the country and its people.

ESSENTIAL FACTS

OFFICIAL NAME: ITALIAN REPUBLIC

GEOGRAPHY

Area: 116,348 square miles (301,340 sq km)

Highest Elevation: Mont Blanc at 15,577 feet (4,748 m)

Lowest Elevation: Mediterranean Sea at 0 feet (0 m)

PEOPLE

Population: 61.1 million (2022 est.)

Most Populous City: Rome (4.298 million)

Ethnic Groups: Mostly Italian; also other

Religions: Christianity, Islam, Judaism, unaffiliated

GOVERNMENT

Type of Government: Parliamentary republic

Capital: Rome

Head of State: President

Head of Government: Prime minister

Legislature: Bicameral, with a Senate and a Chamber of Deputies

ECONOMY

Currency: Euro

Major Industries: Tourism, iron and steel, clothing, footwear, auto manufacturing

Natural Resources: Marble, pumice, pozzolana, feldspar

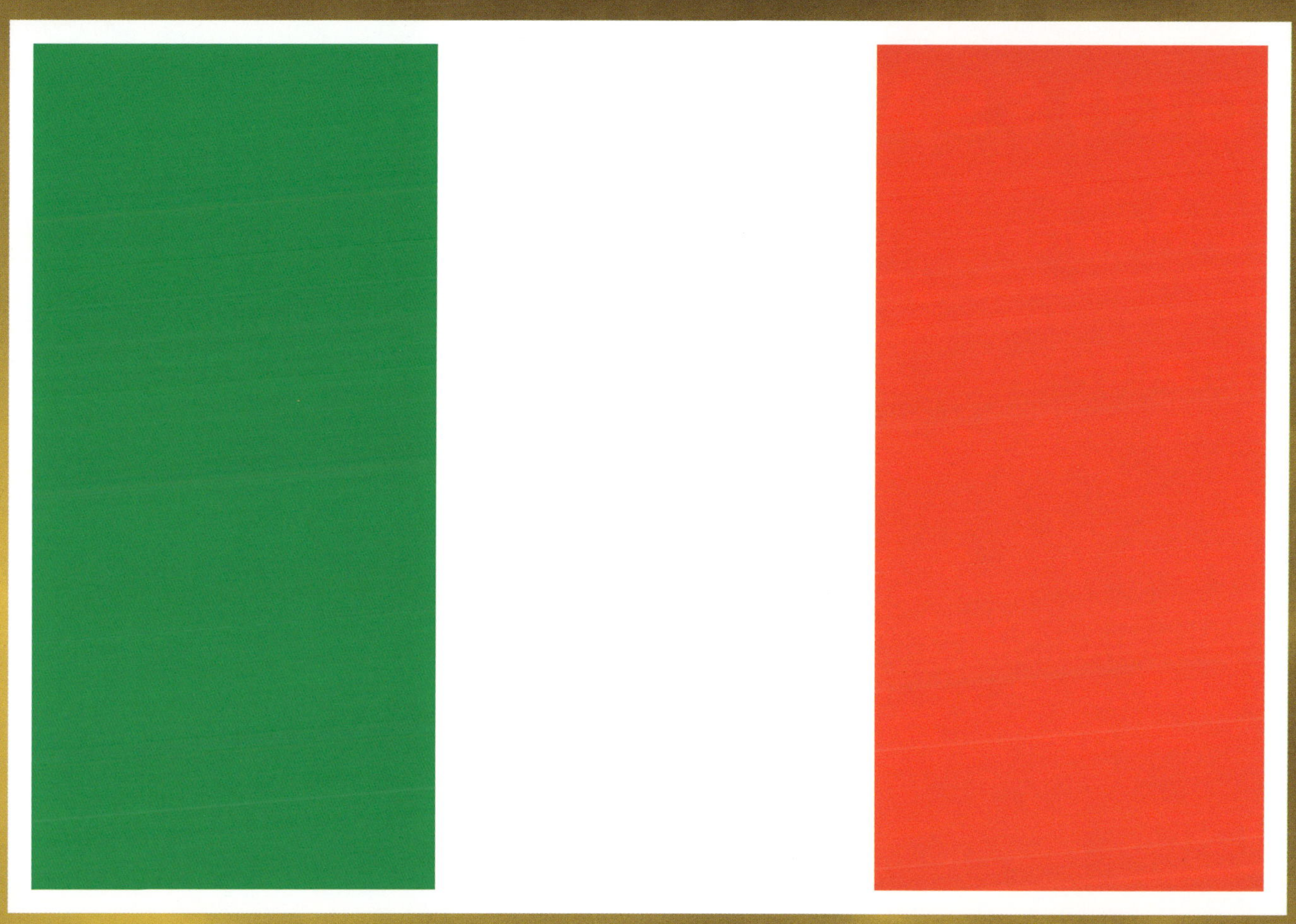

NATIONAL SYMBOLS

National Anthem: "Il Canto degli Italiani" ("The Song of the Italians")

National Bird: Italian sparrow

National Flower: White lily

GLOSSARY

AMPHITHEATER
A round or oval arena without a roof, surrounded by seats, and used for outdoor events.

AQUEDUCT
A pipe or channel built to carry water over a long distance.

BIOME
A community of plants and animals that adapt to and live in a specific climate.

CONSERVATION
Purposeful, planned preservation and protection of wildlife and their habitats from exploitation or destruction.

EXPORT
To sell goods to another country.

FASCIST
A government having a powerful leader who puts the needs of the country over the freedoms of individual citizens.

GLADIATOR
A person engaged in a fight to the death as public entertainment for ancient Romans.

IMPORT
To buy goods from another country.

INDUSTRIALIZED
Shifted from a mainly agricultural economy to one based on manufacturing of goods.

OBELISK
A tall, four-sided, narrow, tapering monument that ends in a pyramid-like shape at the top.

PARTISAN
A member of an armed group formed to fight secretly against an occupying force.

PATRON SAINT
A saint who is said to protect a specific place, activity, person, or thing.

SEDGE
A grasslike plant with triangular stems that grows typically in wet ground.

TRIBUTARY
A stream or river feeding a larger stream, river, or lake.

ADDITIONAL **RESOURCES**

SELECTED BIBLIOGRAPHY

"Italy." *CIA World Factbook*, 11 Apr. 2022, cia.gov. Accessed 14 Apr. 2022.

King, Russell L. "Italy." *Encyclopedia Britannica*, 13 Apr. 2022, britannica.com. Accessed 14 Apr. 2022.

Riches, Christopher, and Peter Stalker. *A Guide to Countries of the World*. Oxford University Press, 2016.

FURTHER READINGS

Carothers, Thomas. *Juventus FC*. Abdo, 2018.

Hamen, Susan E. *Fighting COVID-19 Abroad*. Abdo, 2022.

Hirschmann, Kris. *The Buried City of Pompeii*. ReferencePoint, 2020.

ONLINE RESOURCES

To learn more about Italy, please visit **abdobooklinks.com** or scan this QR code. These links are routinely monitored and updated to provide the most current information available.

MORE INFORMATION

For more information on this subject, contact or visit the following organizations:

European Union
european-union.europa.eu/index_en
The EU is a political and economic alliance of European countries, including Italy. The EU
was formed to improve and strengthen economic and political cooperation in Europe
after World War II.

Uffizi Gallery Museum
Piazzale degli Uffizi 6
50122
Florence, Italy
uffizi.it/en/the-uffizi
Located in Florence, the Uffizi Gallery hosts works of art by great Italian artists such as
Botticelli, Giotto, Cimabue, Michelangelo, Leonardo da Vinci, and Raphael.

Vatican Museums
Viale Vaticano
00165
Rome
museivaticani.va/content/museivaticani/en.html
The Vatican Museums website features information about such sites as the Sistine
Chapel, the Gregorian Egyptian Museum, and the Chapel of Urban VIII.

SOURCE **NOTES**

CHAPTER 1. A TOUR OF ITALY

1. "Colosseum." *Civitatis*, n.d., rome.net. Accessed 27 June 2022.
2. "Colosseum," *Civitatis*.
3. "Colosseum," *Civitatis*.
4. "New Seven Wonders." *CBS News*, 9 June 2007, cbsnews.com. Accessed 27 June 2022.
5. "Leaning Tower of Pisa." *Encyclopedia Britannica*, n.d., britannica.com. Accessed 27 June 2022.
6. "Leaning Tower of Pisa." *Leaning Tower of Pisa*, n.d., towerofpisa.org. Accessed 27 June 2022.
7. "Leaning Tower of Pisa," *Encyclopedia Britannica*.
8. "An Ancient History, a Timeless Passion." *Casale Marchese*, n.d., casalemarchese.it. Accessed 27 June 2022.
9. "Italy." *CIA World Factbook*, 2022, cia.gov. Accessed 27 June 2022.
10. "Italy Population." *Worldometer*, 26 July 2022, worldometers.info. Accessed 26 July 2022.

CHAPTER 2. GEOGRAPHY

1. "Italy." *CIA World Factbook*, 2022, cia.gov. Accessed 27 June 2022.
2. "Italy," *CIA World Factbook*.
3. "Italy," *CIA World Factbook*.
4. "France." *CIA World Factbook*, 2022, cia.gov. Accessed 27 June 2022.
5. "Land of Italy." *Encyclopedia Britannica*, n.d., britannica.com. Accessed 27 June 2022.
6. "The Dolomites." *UNESCO*, n.d., whc.unesco.org. Accessed 27 June 2022.
7. "Drainage of Italy." *Encyclopedia Britannica*, n.d., britannica.com. Accessed 27 June 2022.
8. "Drainage of Italy," *Encyclopedia Britannica*.
9. "Lake Garda." *Encyclopedia Britannica*, n.d., britannica.com. Accessed 27 June 2022.
10. Danielle Hill. "What Are Some Unique Landforms in Italy?" *USA Today*, 26 Jan. 2018, traveltips.usatoday.com. Accessed 27 June 2022.
11. "Sicily." *Encyclopedia Britannica*, n.d., britannica.com. Accessed 27 June 2022.
12. "The Dreamy Islands Where Italians Go to Escape." *AFAR*, 29 Mar. 2022, afar.com. Accessed 27 June 2022.
13. "Geography of Italy." *Understanding Italy*, n.d., understandingitaly.com. Accessed 27 June 2022.
14. "Italy," *CIA World Factbook*.
15. "Italy: Current Climate." *World Bank Group*, n.d., climateknowledgeportal.worldbank.org. Accessed 27 June 2022.
16. "Average Temperatures for Italy in July." *Current Results*, n.d., currentresults.com. Accessed 27 June 2022.

CHAPTER 3. PLANTS AND ANIMALS

1. Timothy L. Gall and Derek M. Gleason. "Italy." *Worldmark Encyclopedia of the Nations*, 2012, link.gale.com. Accessed 27 June 2022.

2. Amber Pariona. "Italy's Most Threatened Mammals." *World Atlas*, 29 July 2019, worldatlas.com. Accessed 27 June 2022.

3. Lorenzo Brenna. "5 Species You Can Only Admire in Italy." *Lifegate*, 3 Mar. 2015, lifegate.com. Accessed 27 June 2022.

4. "Sicilian Fir." *IUCN Red List*, 15 Mar. 2016, iucnredlist.org. Accessed 27 June 2022.

5. "Golden Eagle." *Encyclopedia Britannica*, n.d., britannica.com. Accessed 27 June 2022.

6. Pariona, "Italy's Most Threatened Mammals," *World Atlas*.

7. Pariona, "Italy's Most Threatened Mammals," *World Atlas*.

8. Pariona, "Italy's Most Threatened Mammals," *World Atlas*.

9. "Mediterranean Monk Seal." *Marine Mammal Commission*, n.d., mmc.gov. Accessed 27 June 2022.

10. "Italy." *IUCN Red List*, n.d., iucnredlist.org. Accessed 27 June 2022.

11. Pariona, "Italy's Most Threatened Mammals," *World Atlas*.

12. Pariona, "Italy's Most Threatened Mammals," *World Atlas*.

13. Amber Pariona. "The National Parks of Italy." *World Atlas*, 29 July 2019, worldatlas.com. Accessed 27 June 2022.

14. Emily Heber. "Restoration on Italian Islands, It's about Saving Seabirds." *Island Conservation*, 6 Aug. 2020, islandconservation.org. Accessed 27 June 2022.

15. Heber, "Restoration on Italian Islands," *Island Conservation*.

CHAPTER 4. HISTORY

1. John Noble Wilford. "Fossil Teeth Put Humans in Europe Earlier than Thought." *New York Times*, 2 Nov. 2011, nytimes.com. Accessed 27 June 2022.

2. "Map of Vatican City State." *Nations Online*, n.d., nationsonline.org. Accessed 27 June 2022.

3. "Research Starters: Worldwide Deaths in World War II." *The National WWII Museum*, n.d., nationalww2museum.org. Accessed 27 June 2022.

CHAPTER 5. PEOPLE AND CULTURE

1. Benjamin Elisha Sawe. "Largest Ethnic Groups of Italy." *World Atlas*, 18 July 2019, worldatlas.com. Accessed 27 June 2022.

2. "Demographic Trends." *Encyclopedia Britannica*, n.d., britannica.com. Accessed 27 June 2022.

3. Timothy L. Gall and Derek M. Gleason. "Italy." *Worldmark Encyclopedia of the Nations*, 2012, link.gale.com. Accessed 27 June 2022.

4. "The Top 5 Operas Played in the World." *Opera Lirica di Roma*, n.d., operaliricaroma.it. Accessed 27 June 2022.

5. "Milan Fashion Week." *Fashion United*, n.d., fashionunited.com. Accessed 27 June 2022.

6. "Soccer in Italy—A Look at the Culture and History of Italy's Most Popular Sport." *Global Team Events*, n.d., globalteamevents.com. Accessed 27 June 2022.

7. Sourav Das. "Top 10 Most Successful Italian Football Clubs of All Time." *Sports Browser*, 2 Mar. 2022, sportsbrowser.net. Accessed 27 June 2022.

8. Das, "Top 10 Most Successful Italian Football Clubs," *Sports Browser*.

CHAPTER 6. POLITICS

1. "The North Atlantic Treaty." *NATO*, 4 Apr. 1949, nato.int. Accessed 15 Aug. 2022.

2. "Military Personnel in Italy 2010–2021." *Statista*, 26 Aug. 2021, statista.com. Accessed 28 June 2022.

3. Elisabeth Braw. "Italy Is a Quiet Pillar of NATO's Aerial Policing." *Defense One*, 20 Feb. 2022, defenseone.com. Accessed 28 June 2022.

CHAPTER 7. ECONOMICS

1. "Italy: Economy." *globalEDGE*, n.d., globaledge.msu.edu. Accessed 28 June 2022.

2. "Italy." *CIA World Factbook*, 2022, cia.gov. Accessed 28 June 2022.

3. "Italy: Economy," *globalEDGE*.

4. "Tourism in Italian Cities—Statistics & Facts." *Statista*, 12 May 2022, statista.com. Accessed 28 June 2022.

5. "Italy: Economy," *globalEDGE*.

6. "Italy: Economy," *globalEDGE*.

7. Timothy L. Gall and Derek M. Gleason. "Italy." *Worldmark Encyclopedia of the Nations*, 2012, link.gale.com. Accessed 28 June 2022.

8. Philipp Heimberger and Nikolaus Kowall. "Draghi Government: Seven 'Surprising' Facts about Italy." *Vienna Institute for International Economic Studies*, 16 Feb. 2021, wiiw.ac.at. Accessed 28 June 2022.

9. "Italy: Economy," *globalEDGE*.

10. Gall and Gleason, "Italy."

11. "Simplon Tunnel." *Encyclopedia Britannica*, n.d., britannica.com. Accessed 28 June 2022.

12. "Italy," *CIA World Factbook*.

13. Alexander Kunst. "Car Ownership in Italy in 2022." *Statista*, 18 May 2022, statista.com. Accessed 28 June 2022.

14. "Italy," *CIA World Factbook*.

CHAPTER 8. ITALY TODAY

1. "University of Bologna." *Encyclopedia Britannica*, n.d., britannica.com. Accessed 28 June 2022.

2. "Arrival in Europe: Italy." *International Rescue Committee*, n.d., rescue.org. Accessed 1 July 2022.

3. "Italian Elections 2018–Full Results." *Guardian*, 5 Mar. 2018, theguardian.com. Accessed 1 July 2022.

4. "Russia Puts the Gas Squeeze on France and Italy." *Politico*, 17 June 2022, politico.eu. Accessed 1 July 2022.

5. "Aging Population of Italy–Statistics & Facts." *Statista*, 9 Sep. 2021, statista.com. Accessed 1 July 2022.

ABOUT THE **AUTHOR**

CARLA MOONEY

Carla Mooney is a graduate of the University of Pennsylvania with a degree in economics. Today, she writes for young people and is the author of many books for young adults and children. Mooney enjoys traveling to new places around the world.